ISBN 978-1-331-76067-2
PIBN 10231164

Forgotten Books is a registered trademark of FB &c Ltd.
Copyright © 2018 FB &c Ltd.
FB &c Ltd, Dalton House, 60 Windsor Avenue, London, SW19 2RR.
Company number 08720141. Registered in England and Wales.

For support please visit www.forgottenbooks.com

1 MONTH OF
FREE
READING

at

www.ForgottenBooks.com

By purchasing this book you are eligible for one month membership to ForgottenBooks.com, giving you unlimited access to our entire collection of over 1,000,000 titles via our web site and mobile apps.

To claim your free month visit:

www.forgottenbooks.com/free231164

English
Français
Deutsche
Italiano
Español
Português

www.forgottenbooks.com

Mythology Photography **Fiction**
Fishing Christianity **Art** Cooking
Essays Buddhism Freemasonry
Medicine **Biology** Music **Ancient
Egypt** Evolution Carpentry Physics
Dance Geology **Mathematics** Fitness
Shakespeare **Folklore** Yoga Marketing
Confidence Immortality Biographies
Poetry **Psychology** Witchcraft
Electronics Chemistry History **Law**
Accounting **Philosophy** Anthropology
Alchemy Drama Quantum Mechanics
Atheism Sexual Health **Ancient History**
Entrepreneurship Languages Sport
Paleontology Needlework Islam
Metaphysics Investment Archaeology
Parenting Statistics Criminology
Motivational

OTHER NOTES

BY

MARY BOOLE HINTON

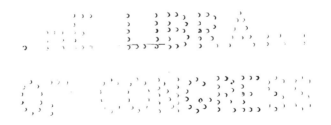

WASHINGTON, D. C.:

THE NEALE PUBLISHING COMPANY

431 Eleventh Street

MCMI

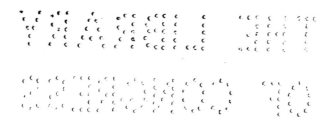

TO MY HUSBAND

"THE Quest After Music" originally appeared in the *Atlantic*, "Root and Rose" in *Harper's Magazine*, "Body and Spirit" in *The Sunday School Times*, "Any Daughter to Any Mother" in *The Outlook*, and are republished in this volume by kind permission.

M. B. H.

Errata.

Thought- Line Six.
    For needst read <u>needest</u>.

In Rapport with a Butterfly- Line Se
    For Beauteous wight read <u>radian</u>

A Laburnum in October- Line Ten.
    For passions's read <u>passion's</u>.

The Little Poet- Line Twenty three.
    For tunes read <u>tune</u>.

Sonnet on the Petrarchan- Line Eight
    For you read <u>ye</u>.

Decision- Line Fifteen.
    For As we choose read As we cho

                    Punctuation.

Nature's Notes- Line Sixteen.
    No period after "Own"

Midsummer- Line Eleven.
    No period after "drowned"

CONTENTS

The Quest After Music

A voice, a voice is calling through the night.
Sleepers, awaken! Get each one his light,
His woodman's axe to cleave the undergrowth
Of claspèd boughs to human entry loath,
His keen-wrought sword to fight with savage foe,
His fair-rigged skiff to cross where rivers flow.

'T were like the rush of feet from diverse ways
Where men have seen a distant city blaze.

A voice, a voice is calling through the night.
Some being calls! Our fathers judged aright
Who peopled sound of wave and song of wind
With multitudinous things of spirit kind.
Some being calls! Some being hides within
The magic tuning of the violin,
The glad rejoicing of the golden horn,
The hautbois mournful as a ghost forlorn,
The cymbal's sweep that mocks a wild typhoon,
The gentle flute, the harp, the deep bassoon.

Some being calls! and they, the called, are blest
Who yield their lives unto a fruitless quest,
Who still pursuing have not cried ''Too late!''
Till Music finds them dead beside her gate.

The Yellow Trumpet

(At the Banda Rossa)

A lake of sound.   O'er leaning thence
The yellow trumpet looked at me
Corolla-wise, rememberingly.

Dreamful, reproachful gaze intense :
" You are of us.   Come back," it said,
" To music and to maidenhead."

Love-bound I would not hie me hence.
Yet wan-hope toil more heartsome grew
Because the yellow trumpet knew.

Thought

All thought at birth, at birth,
Is some one's love or pain
Chilled journeying through the brain,
Frore—lifeless—come to earth.

Cold crystal ! thee I touch.
Thou needst not flinch, close-pressed.
In thee the hurrying passions rest,
That clamored overmuch.

Sons of the Morning

All the sons of the morning sang for gladness.
Homer, Virgil, and thou, revered Catullus,
Masters are ye with dread averted faces.

All the sons of the morning sang for gladness.
Who of poets will tell me what that song was?
Who of harpers retone its voiceless music?

Like a soul that has sinned beyond redemption,
Like the fruit-of-the-womb that dies untimely,
Thus I perish, I faint afar from wisdom.

Dree my heart is that thirsts for classic fountains.
Deserts climbing to touch the dim horizon
Close up round me and suck me down in silence.

Hark!   With murmur of distant deathless voices,
Lo, the sons of the morning hail me friendly.
Great their dole is for outcast fellow singers.

The Pearl Diver

There was agelong gloom in the coralled caves,
　　Where the veil of a turbulent sea
Did hide all else save the oarweed frond
　　By the barrier reef trailed free.

No hope from the dip of the curlew's wing,
　　The stare of the cold white star.
What bodeth it, then, that a storm-spent sail
　　Is afloat on the waters afar?

The diver leaned out o'er the stern of the boat,
　　And he murmured in tremulous tone:
"O, dark, dark depths, there are pearls in you;
　　Be comforted—I have known."

Revery

Just such a sound as makes us think—How Still!
    Just such a silence that we whisper—Hark!
And wait some voice to come; entranced the will;
    The light all vanished though it is not dark.
Just such a wakening that our dream thoughts cling
    And seem to plead: '' We *could* pass if we would.''
Trembles unearthly fantasy—takes wing—
    Wooed hence unto a deeper solitude.

Any Daughter to Any Mother

In bitter pangs the babe was borne ;
    By greater pangs the child was reared.
Not yet the mother's heart, though torn,
    Was scarred and seared.

But will left will dividing far ;
    'Tis written in the book of fate
That each must follow his own star,
    And all must wait.

Mother, in thine a mother's hand
    Is clasped to-day across the years.
In the great hand of God we stand,
    And smile through tears.

En Rapport With a Butterfly

Far out above the wistful wave,
　Now up the woodland hill,
Then far, far out, thy tired wings
　Fly on—and weakening still
Fly on, fly on, a sorrowing flight ;
　Nor mayest thou understand
How yearningly I watch thy way—
　He hasteth to my hand.

How exquisite the clinging of
　His little, little feet.
Oh! life's a field-of-cloth-of-gold
　Where fellow kings may meet.
And we are kings in comradeship,
　Thou wind-borne winged one fair.
My heart returned from following thee
　To find thee harbored there.

Stay, stay awhile thou beauteous wight !
　Whom love hath lured to me,
Whom very love hath made my own;
　What Morrow-guest shall be
If ghoul-like thoughts with furtive steps
　Blackhooded from the light
Slink down the stairway of my soul
　And peer into the night !

Love Song

Hath anyone taken the bloom off
  Thy love for me?
Is it entire and single
  On thy life's tree?.
No one has taken the bloom off
  My love for thee.
It is as God first grew it
  On my life's tree.
One little bud he set there,
  Green veiled from sight.
Followed a pure white blossom,
  Thy heart's delight.
Soon the red fruit must ripen
  In summer sun.
May the bloom blush on forever
  Till life is done.

A Laburnum in October

One tree a blaze of blossom glowing glory-crowned.
Nature, disrobing for her winter sleep, the ground
With withered leaves, her garments cast aside, doth
    strew.
Here only is there left the pleasaunce summer knew :
Here only, desolation loiters in its quest.
Thou tremulous thing of fire, I would upon my
    breast
Some sacred type of joy's eternity enfold :
Give me a branch ! So, swift athwart the dewy wold
With eager hasting steps to touch the tree I went.

Love, Love, when thy first passions's burning
    breath is spent
No Yellow Leaves bear thou where gold-heart
    bloom should cling.
For I have faith, and there will come another Spring.

The Little Poet

A little poet singing down the lane—
(Forgotten childhood come thou back again)
A volume clasped against her heart with glee.
What secret hidest thou from the world and me?
This darling book my darling verse shall keep,
And I may safely leave it while I sleep.
Oh may the script within be ever fair,
And gracious fancies, only, written there.
My little poet, all your themes were then
Of God and nature and heroic men.
The love of Christ illumed your childish eyes.
A radiance gleamed from hills and seas and skies.
But now the smoke of unforgiven wrongs
Has lived to cloud and blacken all your songs.
No lark may pipe athwart the stainèd page,
No flower may bloom, and no enraptured sage
Brave death for right—where lost in gloom profound,
The broken timbrel drags along the ground.
Return, bright faith, return—as rivers flow
From far off heights through sunlit meads below.
A bitter heart will jar the sweetest lyre.
And who would save for Art his gift entire
Must tune the soul—howe'er he tunes the strings—
When inspiration lifts her brooding wings.

Requiescat

Closer, closer clasp the earth mound.
   Be the head down prest.
      That's his breast !
Should a wandering grass stalk stray
On the upper cheek this way,
That's the lappel over-folded ;
     Let it stay.

He's so near.
You have only to dig deep
Were it not you fear
The night blackness while men sleep.
He's so far.
There is no footway to that land
On moon or sun or star,
Where angel children quarrel for his hand.

Hush ! sob softly—lest that voice divine
Speaking you the grand, white samite line
    Should be forgot.
Hush ! for the words make tune.
Hush ! He will come quite soon.
   But tell it—not.
     Tell—it—not.

In Far Japan

A moss-lined wayside well.
Bright tufts, therein, of pink begonia smiled.
First time to see begonia growing wild
    Were joy no tongue could tell.

Shall rude barbaric hands
Play havoc, ruthless, leaving bare wet stone
Harsh outlined where the little clump had grown
    Agirt with tendril bands?

Bear home thy treasure:
Greed dies, the whilst regret is slowly born
That any living thing should be so torn
    For our poor pleasure.

Dear little plant and brave,
Thy wrongs are over and my sin is past.
Such mood of desecration be my last
    This side the grave.

Root and Rose

Such roots, good folk, can never bear a rose.
Yea, we have sworn it.   Let the blossom bloom.
We righteous will not wot thereof, to whom
    A rose it shall not be on roots like those.

Body and Spirit

He was thinking a thought when he died.
  As his soul slipped the leash from her place,
A moment the thought dallied backward
  To write itself onto his face.

Flesh of flesh, burning to ashes,
  Body, crumbling to dust,
Hold for the High God his secret,
  Mouldering be true to thy trust.

For earth in her dreams hath no treasure,
  Nor heaven in her heights—to compare
. With the glory of buried ideals,
  Heart-longings, a tear and a prayer.

The Hermit

(A Japanese Picture)

Creatures of clay he takes and wind swept leaves
    That fall about his feet.
He breathes thereon the breath of life, nor grieves
    When, fearlessly and fleet,

They pass beyond him, faring to their kind.
    Yea, these, who are his own
Yet are not freely his, he will not bind,
    But lives and dies alone.

What guerdon hath he then for given-life ?
    Ask only such as he—
Sin bearers, sorrow touched for human strife,
    Whose mood is mystery.

Life and Song

Stay, Poet, if thy griefs were grief,
   The words according well
Would die unuttered on thy lips,
   Nor any tale would tell
Sad kinsman of the soulless god
   That sighs in hollow shell.

Nay, rather, if my griefs be grief,
   The words according well,
Must pour impassioned from my lips
   Their wildest tale to tell.
The sorrows of the morning are
   The songs of Vesper Bell.

Too Close to the Music

Too close to the music—then crawl
   Like a blindworm avoiding the light
Round yon ledge in the rear of the hall.
   Hang over and hear it aright.

Too close? What's that strange phrase of thine?
   Ask the man with his hand on the drum
If *he* flinch, if *he* swerve out of line
   Lest the tone-beats his brain should benumb.

From the depths of that whirlpool of sound
   Comes a voiceless but terrible cry,
While the harmonies eddy around :
   '' More close, even yet, and more nigh.''

Then a forward lean of the life
   And a forward tilt of the soul
Till we joy in the shriek of the fife,
   Till there's a rapture where trumpet blasts roll.

'Tis not Fear that shall claim us at last.
   As we kneel at thy feet to adore,
Mighty Song, draw us close, dangers past,
   To thy wonderful heart evermore.

A Notebook of Auld Lang Syne

Half smilingly, in reverie mood,
    I con these pages o'er,
Until the soul-life of a child
    Becomes my soul once more.

Athrill with weird imaginings,
    See, here the wan script runs :
"A thousand sun-lit gods beneath
    A thousand god-lit suns."

Old rhymes, wherein the language lilt
    Glides twirling from the sense,
Ye have a strange new meaning, fraught
    With deepest consequence.

I'm harking for my sun-lit gods
    That crooned, yon far-off day.
What dire enchantment me beguiled
    To weep long years away?

The earth's atremble with their tread.
    I greet them, glad and strong.
Heart's temple (altar, choir, and crypt),
    Grows vibrant by their song.

Out of Tune

Hear how the sense doth shrink
As from a crèvasse brink
   At the slightest swerve in tone.
Seemeth a wizard hidden
Dabbleth in things forbidden
Save to the Gods alone.

Hence must my spirit cry
For music as on high
   That knoweth no mortal bond ;
Loosed from the scale of seven
Wing through the heights of Heaven,
   Find the beyond.

Nature's Notes

There's a lilt, lilt, lilt of falling water,
  There's a tune, tune, tune of falling sound.
There's a dream, dream, dream of mystic music,
  Ghost-like, crossing mortal bound.
There's a lilt, lilt, lilt of falling water,
  There's a tune, tune, tune of falling sound.

There's a trill, trill, trill of bird musicians,
  But 'tis hard to find the key;
Half caressing and half mocking
  Is their challenge tossed to me.
There's a trill, trill, trill of bird musicians,
  But 'tis hard to find the key.

There's a sigh, sigh, sigh of winds that soaring
  Search the heights and deeps of tone.   .
I hear them following, following nature's notes
  That yet shall be my own.
When my spirit goes exploring
  All the heights and deeps of tone.

Sonnet on the Petrarchan

The Octave is a dive into the deep
Whose long, long moment hurryeth after Light ;
An arrow perilously poised for flight
The grievèd hand constraining scarce may keep ;
A whirlpool dallying in its central sleep
Ere yet the tangent tides fling forth their might.
Up-gathered forces—lost to sound and sight,
Where e'er you are your prisonment I weep.

In glory as of myriad falling stars
Loosed be the sextet from all bonds and bars,
Primordial Impulse greatened through control.
Thee will I worship in thy straightmost laws
Sonnet of sonnets, deathlessly—because
Thy story is the story of my soul.

A Last Confession

You ask me why I did not take the veil,
  Though all my life had set my heart thereon :
Why ere I came within the convent's pale
  A lower impulse won ;

Why I forsook the Lord and His dear ways
  For human loves, for earthly joys and sin ;
And why I now am come to end my days
  This holy place within.

It was a vision that I saw which broke
  The cherished purpose of my virgin years—
Small grabbling hands and mournful eyes that spoke
  Albeit dimmed by tears.

And labyrinthine curves of golden hair—
  A pure, sweet forehead floating down beside—
Ah, me ! the face was marvelously fair—
  In awful doubt, I cried:

" My son that is to be ! What *right* have I
  To rob thee of thy passion to be born,"
Not though I shrive my soul in agony,
  The body scourged and torn.

"Unconscious will, whose fires of life are lit
  With longing that my flesh may be thy home
Till thou hereafter breaking forth from it
  In light of days to come,

"And girding on the stature of a man,
    Wilt need no longer woman's wistful care—
I vow to end my days where I began—
    In love and faith and prayer."

So spake I, and so acted out—but now
    My husband's spirit with my God's is blent—
And that is well—death-dews creep o'er my brow—
    My length of days is spent.

———

The Future of Ivan Ivanovitch

Ivan Ivanovitch, the Terrible!
        A woman sinned through sudden fright.
        He struck her soul into the night.
The bleeding body, headless, knelt on still.
By shedding of the blood he changed the will.
How must she love him in the life to be
With higher visions of eternity;
And honor him, and ever count him friend,
If he but make her holy in the end!

Ivan Ivanovitch, the Just!
        A soul may sin, but not through fright.
        A soul may sin for sin's delight.
Hence, haply while the hand well poised dealt death,
Swift thoughts sped spaceward, borne by dying
        breath—
"On these foundations, well and truly laid,
He shall upbear the standard he has made.
On him, on him may fall the wrath divine,
Should he condone a greater sin than mine."

29

Midsummer

Sea Sand:
    I touch thee.
Thou burnest my hand.
    So joy would burn.

Sea Wrack:
    I feel thee.
Pikelets pierce back.
    So doth sorrow pierce.

Sea Sound:
    I salute thee.
Chanting the requiem of the drowned.
    Chant my requiem.

The Seer

I came to him, kneeling; I asked of him then:
    Would you die?
Your life ebbs out for men.

But a heart-throb sang in the tones of the sea:
    Ah, why
Does the world bring its love-life to me?

Idolatry

What hast thou done, little maiden,
  Wonderful little maid!
Hast taken the gods of the heathen
  To be thy dolly instead?

Terrible gods come acrushing
  The sensuous human soul;
Not to thy hurt, my childling,
  ^ Do the wheels of juggernaut roll.

There! Sit thee down on the trackway
  And croon thy dolly a song;
Let the procession sweep by thee,
  Queenling, whom none may wrong.

Nor shalt thou wrong thine own spirit,
  So this commandment thou heed:
"Curb the wild impulse of worship,
  Mothering human need."

Prelude and Reverie

This rock becomes a little isle
  Encircled by the sea,
Where fancy's dreaming heart may rest
  And fancy's thoughts flow free.

Dip, sea-shell, dip—a cup of love,
  How salt so e'er it be,
While Lucy in the Isle of Man
  Another drinks to me.

REVERIE.

We, side by side,
  Half turn the head
  For inward dread
  An empty space may give the lie
  When spirits know each other nigh.

Still side by side,
  Whose fingers silt the sand,
  Whom seas on seas divide.

We, side by side,
  Hand never touching hand,
  Nor voice aye echoing speech,
  Endlessly out of reach,
  Remote as star from star.

Answer this question, dear:
  What is it *to be far?*
  What is it *to be near?*

The Keltic Magic

(A sonnet on the sonnet.)

Tell me the story of thy during heart,
    Mage Merlin! 'Mid the drowse of Keltic dreams
    Ancestral censors swing from carven beams.
Prayer-wise, aswoon, I vision what thou art.
Oft in my visioning the tears down start.
    Oft as I track thee in my quest, meseems
    Lamp-like and tremulant the Oak-bole gleams.
Worlds must not hear us where we talk apart!

Weird from his eerie crypt the Sonnet sings:
I have no likeness with material things,
    Nor pearl, nor casket, nor the blown seashell.
Locked is my secret while the words go by,
For understanding darkens to a cry.
    Child of the Kelt,—thou knowest; thou knowest
      me well.

Credo

Thought-wise my soul's agnostic in its trend,
But music-wise, is mystic to the end.
Bare lies the shrine, safe guarded from belief.
Ramparts are vain.   Let song, however brief,
Light in her farings near the altar stone.
'Tis rife with gods ! 'tis vibrant, star-bestrown.

Election

All love not Thee, O Christ, who truly love.
Helpless the harp-like spirit of the child
Awaits some call divine.   Who comes too late
This quest must lose.   Who comes betimes may win
The worshipper Thou, Jesus, didst not claim.
No Hell, therefore, no Heaven ; but after death
Each goes to his own gods and is content.

The Serpent on the Hearth

(The woman speaks.)

What is that lying on the hearth?
    So cold, so cold, so cold.
  A babe that sleeps—my God, will it never wake?
What is that lying on the hearth?
    So cold, so cold, so cold.
  Stone imaged—still—my God, 'tis a rattlesnake!

Strange comrades, these, upon one hearth—
    A serpent and my child—
      My undefiled.

Ho! serpent of the glistening eyes,
    That charm to slay.
  For you the forest vast,
  Fate's horoscope has cast.
    For me the hearth so small,
      Which was my all.

I have not hurt you in your place!
    Did I or any dear one stray
      Your way
    I had not said you nay,
      But bowed before you in life's race.
  For you the forest lands are wild.
    But yet you came upon my hearth!
    But yet you killed my child!

Ho, serpent of the glistening eyes,
  Now darkening, tell me true,
Is there one thing you really love?
      I hold you do.

See, see yon fateful script illume the walls.
The devils know it, pacing fiery halls;
The angels know it, kneeling by the throne—
That motherhood shall be avenged in motherhood
    alone.

Back to your nest, back, back,
And cover up the track.
I'd scorn to spy upon you as you pass.
You'll hear my feet crush the dried grass.

      (The serpent speaks.)

For me the brake, the bight!
      Thou woman wight,
      It vanisheth;
It dwindleth as a trail
Upon the sands;
      And death breeds death.
Sick are the forest lands.
None knoweth the might of human eyes:
      Who feels them dies.
The shrinking forests quail
      And close about
The shuddering shapes within
      That are my kin.
Lost rivers call us from without.

Thine, thine the hearth so small!
Who hath the hearth hath all.
Erewhilst one firelight ray
Enkindled yesterday,
Behold it shimmer on the golden corn,
Torch light of generations yet unborn.

Man's child, thou heir of Heaven and hell,
Primordial monsters cry, entombed:
"The chosen shall not curse the doomed."
    Farewell! Farewell!

Life

  This pencil pleaseth me not,
    For it lacketh the rubber end.
  My lines stray wide;
  But the salt teartide
    Doth blear and blot,
  Not righten the crooked trend.
    This pencil pleaseth me not.

Emotion

Emotion is a vice like drink.
    Take heed you do not feel.
Jerk off high dreaming in a twink,
    If through the soul it steal.
Some erring temper-gust, forthright
Proves you a hypocrite.

Elizabethan Lyric

Calm and still, calm and still,
Wandereth my soul at will
　　Through the upper sphere.
Sad and slow, sad and slow,
Toileth on my flesh below
　　In the darkness here.

Not to me, not to me,
Is there rest eternally,
　　Free from impulse strange.
For my peace, for my peace,
Waning starlike it shall cease,
　　Fading it shall change.

So my grief, so my grief,
Maketh its abiding brief,
　　Yea, and tarryeth not.
But my love, but my love,
Fixèd is as light above,
　　Though all else forgot.

Moods

Two moods dispart my soul.
　　Today which shall it be—
The mood of bitterness ?
　　The mood of reverie ?
Lord, Thou hast bid me *fail*.
　　My duties broken lie
Under the weakening hand,
　　Thou, only, knowest why.
Success without the walls
　　Is haughtily a king.
Night-long mine ears do plaine
　　His cruel blazoning.
Glory my birthright is ;
　　Bereft of earth's delights
The veriest babe up-built
　　A stairway to the heights.
Shall radiant gods down-troop
　　Who sing my soul adream,
Who hourly me baptise
　　A follower of the gleam ?
Then let no-direful thought,
　　No desperate mood of mine,
Be cherished so to wound
　　Those visitants divine.

Two moods dispart my soul
　　Today which shall it be—
The mood of bitterness ?
　　The mood of reverie ?

After Death

(Founded on passage in the Zend Avesta.)

Three long days the righteous soul fleeteth.
As earth dim recedeth, recedeth,
A mystical maiden he meeteth.

Thy good deeds, she saith, gone before thee,
Are quickened in me to adore thee,
Like perfume about thee and o'er thee.

He following, he following, she guiding,
They enter the place of abiding,
The halls of unevil-betiding.

But joy like to thine, O, my poet,
No angel-tongued paean could show it,
No rapt mortal vision foreknow it.

To thee when the world-pageant shifted,
A magical music came drifted—
Thy lyrics in glory uplifted.

Revengefulness

Sins are but Burglars in the house of life
Claiming no favor of the inhabitant.

Bolts must be wrenched and lintels torn away
And armèd conscience, gasping, gagged and bound
Ere wickedness plants foot upon the stair.

What monster sin is this who comes by night,
Hugging his permit from the deathless past?

Aha, my shuddering soul, thou criest: Avaunt!
Yet cans't not choose but sanction,—so thou hear
The scraping of his latch key in the lock.

Personality

Thee, little boat, I erst did guide
With a tow rope dipped athwart the tide,
And tug through harsh canals:
Now down the natural waterfalls
  Of feeling shalt thou go,
  Whose trend was ever so.
What ailed thee, then, before?
  Heighho! the banks have a natural curve,
  The reeds lean out with a natural swerve,
And we are we once more.

The Musician's Nirvana

In the day when the stars shall cease singing, when
    lute, harp and voice
Shall not woo the lulled soul of the singer to rise
    and rejoice—
In the place where I was let men listen with raptu-
    rous ears
To a wonderful sound in the wonderful song of the
    spheres.
Let no mention be made of my name or my deeds
    any more.
Let my speech be the moaning of seas and the cat-
    aract's roar
And the wailing of winds and the strong everlast-
    ing vibration
Of harmonies thrilled through the heights and the
    depths of creation.
Be music my spirit—not mine but her spirit in me;
Be music my worship—for whoso adores her is she.
Soul in anguish, climb out on the resonant blast of
    the horn,
Never more, never more in the wheel of rebirths to
    be born.

Decision

Musing on the bridge he standeth,
    Listeth low and listeth long,
Till the detonating water
    Seems to call him in its song;
Call him, by the wistful heart-love
    Of the sinless for the strong:

"Dreamer—on the bridge of Judgment
    O'er the river's rushing tide—
Keystone sways; the bridge is falling;
    Flee to one or other side.
Are you hero? Are you traitor?
    Soon, Ah, soon the floods divide!"

Still, in passionless compassion
    Welled up words that could not wait:
"As we choose in small things always
    We must choose at last in great;
For 'tis then the gods deny us
    Our own hand upon our fate."

Cadence Song

A yearning for the cadence, for the cadence **at** its
    close
Is the story of all music; and the secret music
    knows
Is a yearning for the cadence, then the cadence at
    its close.

How my heart desires the cadence while the music
    winding flows!
Every inlet, every islet into vivid greenness grows
When my heart desires the cadence while the music
    winding flows.

If my heart desires the cadence as a bee desires the
    rose
Give me, give me *now* the cadence, never waiting
    for the close.
'Tis the cadence that is calling while the winsome
    blossom blows.

Two strong chords, forever chiming, shall they
    bring divine repose?
Shall they rock me in the garden where the god of
    music goes?
Two strong chords, forever chiming, shall they
    bring divine repose?

Nay! there's cloying, Ah! there's cloying in the
    sweetness of the rose

L. of C.

And the only joy eternal is a joy that comes and
    goes.
There is cloying in the sweetness of the music or
    the rose.

Then a yearning for the cadence, for the cadence
    at its close
Is the story of all music ; but the secret *music* knows
Is a *yearning-strain*, alternate with the enraptured
    cadence close !

NOTES

Out of Tune

Music's limitation to twelve notes, out of an infinite number of possible notes, must stimulate an enlightened imagination. "Why, Oh why, that great forbidding?" is the cry of the child when first she comes upon the problem. Hardly may the trained musician find answer for it.

Idolatry

The words doll and idol were formerly, by a fanciful etymology, held to be identical. How mystically does not the little wooden image focus to itself two complementary needs of our nature—something to worship, something to protect. Oft the one impulse runs riot while the other lapses through inanition. So strong is the power of little-motherhood that one might imagine it potent against all harms of soul and body. The awful Juggernaut car ploughs its course through blood ; the maddened votaries cast themselves before it. Yet must the oncoming procession turn aside by reason of a little child.

Cadence Song

Cadence phrases are phrases on which the ear comes to rest. By cadence is here meant the Perfect Cadence, the Tonic chord preceded by the Dominant. Much of the older music, sectionally constructed, derives its charm from the frequent but momentary touching of the key-note. Improvisation, too, oft keeps the ear in suspense hovering about the key-note, suggesting, sounding, quitting. The Cadence Song records the real experiment of a musical child who tried to construct a music that should be all cadence.